# *Above* CAPRICORN

# *Above*
# CAPRICORN

## Aboriginal Biographies from Northern Australia

*Stephen Davis*

Angus&Robertson
An imprint of HarperCollins*Publishers*

*This book is dedicated to*

*my four children, Oliver, Jenny, Samara and Wai Mei,*

*who enjoy the friendship of so many Aboriginal people.*

## An Angus & Robertson Publication

Angus&Robertson, an imprint of
HarperCollins*Publishers*
25 Ryde Road, Pymble, Sydney NSW 2073, Australia
31 View Road, Glenfield, Auckland 10, New Zealand

First published in Australia in 1994

National Library of Australia
Cataloguing-in-Publication data:

Davis, Stephen, 1951– .
    Above Capricorn.

    ISBN 0 207 18000 8.

    [1.] Aborigines, Australian — Biography. [2.] Aborigines,
    Australian — History. [3.] Aborigines, Australian — Social life
    and customs. I. Title.

305.89915

All royalties for this edition were donated to charity to assist work among
disadvantaged Aboriginal people in northern Australia.

Cover photograph by Stephen Davis
Design by Darian Causby
Printed in Hong Kong

9 8 7 6 5 4 3 2 1
97 96 95 94

# CONTENTS

## Acknowledgments

This book has been compiled over a period of many years as my family lived and worked with Aboriginal people throughout Australia. We have enjoyed the support and encouragement of so many people, too numerous to list here. Suffice it to say that each one of the people whose story appears in this book afforded us an unlimited hospitality and friendship that, if it were extended throughout our population, would be a marvellous foil to the racism, resentment and distrust that continues to grow in our communities.

## Publisher's Acknowledgment

Permission has been obtained from the following people for the use of their stories in the compilation of this book:

Toby Pitjara, Jackie Friday, Tom Murray, Felix Holmes, Splinter Harris, Eileen Belia, Mick Wagu, Paddy Roe, James Barripang, Biddy Simon.

## Photographic Credits

Photographs are in page order l (left); r (right); t (top); b (bottom). Unless otherwise stated, all photographs © Stephen Davis. In all other cases, copyright remains with individual photographers or institutions.

Page 19, Conservation Commission of the Northern Territory, photo P. Jarver; p. 39, Conservation Commission of the Northern Territory, photo P. Jarver; p. 46, Tony Ford (b l); p. 51, Bay Picture Library; p. 62, Bay Picture Library; p. 66, Bay Picture Library; p. 94, Conservation Commission of the Northern Territory, photo P. Jarver; p. 107, Conservation Commission of the Northern Territory, photo M. Jenner.

*Front cover: Felix Holmes, senior custodian of the Limilngan tribe.*
*Back cover: Spinifex and granite at a significant site for Aboriginal people in Central Australia.*

# INTRODUCTION

Aboriginal culture in Australia is an oral tradition. In this book, senior respected Aboriginal people tell their story, which will now become a part of Australia's written tradition.

These are real life experiences with which few non-Aboriginal Australians will be familiar. Some experiences, such as those of Eileen Belia working for the missus in the 'big house', are common to many older Aboriginal women. Likewise, many Aboriginal men have been drovers and stockmen with experiences similar to those of Mick Wagu, Felix Holmes and Splinter Harris.

Toby Pitjara's story spans a period from prior to his first European contact, through to the sadness of his later years when he helplessly witnesses the end of his culture's traditions. This sadness is also reflected in Mick Wagu's story.

In the stories of James Barripang, who has been raised in the strong Aboriginal traditions of Arnhem Land, and Biddy Simon, who has fervently pursued the customs of her traditional country on the coast of the Bonaparte Gulf, there is more than hope, there is a cast-iron determination to hang on to the culture and breathe new life into it among younger people.

Jackie Friday, Tom Murray and Paddy Roe are active and renowned teachers of the law, each recounting important principles to be uncompromisingly observed in the conduct of life.

These ten Aboriginal Australians are part of a living heritage that we must not allow to die; to do so would equally diminish every Australian.

*James Barripang*

1

# TOBY PITJARA

Toby Pitjara's father was a senior custodian of the Alyawarra tribe.

Growing up in the sparse country of the Northern Territory's Barkly Tablelands, Toby lived a traditional life in his family group until he first saw Europeans who were droving sheep to settle in the Northern Territory. Toby, who until then had 'lived like a kangaroo', had more and more contact with the Europeans and eventually he took a job on a cattle station. A succession of jobs, including shearing and well sinking, across a number of stations on and surrounding his Alyawarra tribal country, brought Toby to Camooweal where he lived among the Bulangu tribe, learning their traditions.

Now Toby is the only one who still recalls the details of Bulangu traditions.

In the Camooweal camp Toby still sings the songs of the Bulangu — the Flying Fox people of past generations.

This is story from the early days
When my father and mother were young
When there was only the old people
I was only nothing then

No matches then
Only light fire by rubbing sticks together
Eat kangaroo, goanna, porcupine, sugarbag
That's all

Early days
When old people was alive
We were all naked ...
No clothes
We hunt kangaroo, goanna ...
Get wild potato
All that thing
We lived like kangaroo

My father and mother
They just live in bush
Not working on station
Just living like kangaroo

We lived all around this country
All the time in the bush
Just living in grass humpy
That for rain time

No white fella then
They come from England

When I was little
We just wake up in morning
Me and my brother
Two sister too

First thing just get warm
Sit around the fire
Behind windbreak
Eat little bit of tucker
Might be left over

Then start walking about
Looking for tucker
Hunting
Just walking round
My father was good hunter
He was too clever

My father make spear for me
But he die too quick

Die Aboriginal way
Black fella catch him ...
Sing him
Then him die

He wasn't old
But they catch him [kill him]
Catch him black fella way ...
Sneaky way

Come along night time
Pinch him hair, fingernail, something
Make that business [sorcery]
Then catch him
Can't see mark nothing [no mark on body]
Come out blood nothing [no bleeding]
That Aboriginal doctor
Use bone
One round one, one sharp one

*Toby Pitjara*

Then my father get sick
Another Aboriginal come
Him have a look
'Oh, no good', him say
Can't clean him up
Should be wrap him up ...
Sing for him
When he wake up
Do it same again
But nobody do it for my father
They just sneak away
Go walkabout
My father just finish up there [die]

Then they call me up
Ask me what dream I see
'Emu', I tell him
'Ah', they said
So they looking for those emu men
Two emu men
They got them
Finish them up [killed them]
Now all level [even]

My old father was boss for emu
Kurtungurlu for emu
He was working man for emu
Now all finished ...
Level

I been walking around this country ...
Walking round meself
My father been finish up then

I was still young

# OBY PITJARA

No white men then
Everyone foot walk
No ride
Only mailman ride

He coming up from south
Get to Warabri
Then another man take over

Warabri to Stirling Station
Then next man take over

*Soudan Station, western Queensland*

Each night ...
He came beside track,
Little bit of tucker
That's all he need

One time I see that mailman
No horse
He been just footwalk
All the way
I seen it myself

Now we got no father
No granny
No old people
I'm the last one

First time we see white man ...
No cattle
He got only sheep and nanny goat
Every station

Every station
All the station
Only sheep and nanny goat
But we never spear them
We only spear kangaroo and emu

My father too quick
Always get emu
Wait till they feed
Looking for Conkerberry bush
But my father hiding there
They couldn't beat him ...
Too quick
Spear that emu close to bone

I watch him
Teach meself
I watch him
Then sneak up alongside emu meself
And catch him
That early day

Now emu wild
Run away quick
See you and him run off
More easier you get sugarbag [wild honey]

Oh too much sugarbag here
One billycan, two billycan
No time at all

When we get kangaroo, emu ...
We eat everything
Use all of him

When my father sick
Rub that emu fat on him
Rub eye with that fat too ...
Make eye clean

Bush potato ...
Oh, lovely tucker
Not like white fella potato [English potato]
That just little one ...
Poor little bugger
But bush potato biggest one
Not rubbish one
Sweet one

When we make spear ...
We use that mulga wood
Cut a long one

*Toby Pitjara's camp at Camooweal, 1988*

Make fire
Heat up that mulga
Bloodwood and Gidgee
Good for burning
Mulga good for spear
Straighten him up

Make a hook
And tie him on
Tie him on with kangaroo string [sinew]
Then let him dry out

*Alyawarra country,*
*Queensland–Northern Territory border*

Get spinifex wax
Put that stone in [stone spear blade]
Wax all around
Then let him dry up
Stone can't come out then
Good one that
Wax dry up
String from kangaroo leg dry up
Proper spear then
Get him kangaroo and emu

Spear him in side [kidneys]
Or under arm [through heart]
Then him dead, that kangaroo
If you spear him rump,
Then him just trot along
And lay down later ...
Sick
Can't get up on sore leg
But long way you gotta follow.

First time
No white fella here
He come from England
Boat and boat and boat ...
Oh, too many
From England

All the way by boat
Sleeping longa boat
When he get off boat
He say,
'Oh this dry country'

First time I see white man
That longa Frew Station
We all got no clothes
Men, women, everybody

Well we see him that white man
And we reckon him might be debil debil
We been hear about him
Shoot him all our people
Shoot 'em out
All over they been shoot 'em out
Then burn 'em bodies in fire

But pretty soon we bin learn him job
Work for white fella
Cartin' wood
Frew Station ...
That first place my people work

After my father finished up [died]
I went back to my country ...
Alyawarra country
Elkedra [Station]
That my father's country
I wanted to see that country
He grew up on that country
And he was boss from early days

I got a job with Kennedy and Riley
They had Elkedra then
Funny bugger managers them fellas
No money
No swag
Not much beef
Only bone ...
Just living on the bone
Give me no money
Nothing
We just working for nothing

Lot a big job
I been sinking well ...

All that game
Just for little bit johnnycake [damper]
And little bit bone
Family living off bush tucker
But later I was sitting down everywhere
Tennant Creek, Booroloola ...
All fresh country for me
New places

Early days
I been working with old Mac Chalmers ...
Shearing sheep
On MacDonald Downs ...
But him dead now

His son there now
Other son kill himself ...
Motor car accident
And nephew
David Weir
He look after Amaroo Station

Early years that was all our country
Not belong to white fellas then
Just Alyawarra country

Some of our mob there now
Albert, Frank and Slippery Morton
They brothers
All Alyawarra ...
Kangaroo mob

When I came back here
Camooweal
Only one old blackfella left
This Bulangu country
But they all finished up [dead] ...
Clean sweep

*Spinifex country near Mount Isa*

My daughter born MacDonald Downs
She just little when I came back here
I brought my family
Wife, children, whole lot,
Bring 'em here
Bulangu country

Now I'm old
Just sitting down here
Looking after this country
Quiet place now
All blackfella gone now
No more here
Bulangu people all gone
Clean sweep!
Now Alyawarra mob looking after

When I was working at Lake Nash
Working for Charlie Payne
Well blackfella from this country ...
Him all gone then

I used to look after steam engine ...
Longa Lake Nash
Chop wood ...
Cart him wood
Make fire for boiler
Get him number [pressure] ...
100
Then start the engine up ...

Start him longa fire that engine ...
Funny bugger

Some fella engine different now
Start him longa oil
All different now

*Termite mounds and dreaming sites*

But that was my game
Early days then

Ah, that was hard work
Only get paid johnnycake, damper
Maybe get little bit of beef
But not like emu
Emu get fat
Good one that
Early day
But that all gone now

Early day
I used to go to ceremony
Big ceremony at Tennant Creek ...
Seven mile water hole
Jungkuragurra
That proper name
All the old men were there
Big mob
But nothing now

Now, no more business
No more corroboree
Only young people now
Business all finished

Young blokes can mind the place
They got no ceremony ...
Nothing
That country got no law
No law when I'm gone

They can't catch him kangaroo
Only get beef now
They can only just sit on the country
No corroboree

Now I can die anytime
Anytime now
But I should die on my country ...
Elkedra

No one catch him up my number
No one been kill him me
We can't catch him up our country
So I can die now

I had proper name in early days
Aboriginal name
Now they all call me Kwalu Kwalu
But that only name for my country
Round stone place
Look like footballs

Kwalu Kwalu ...
That not my proper name
But I can't get him now [can't remember]
Too old ...
Everybody gone
Can't even get him my own name anymore
Only white fella name ...
Toby.

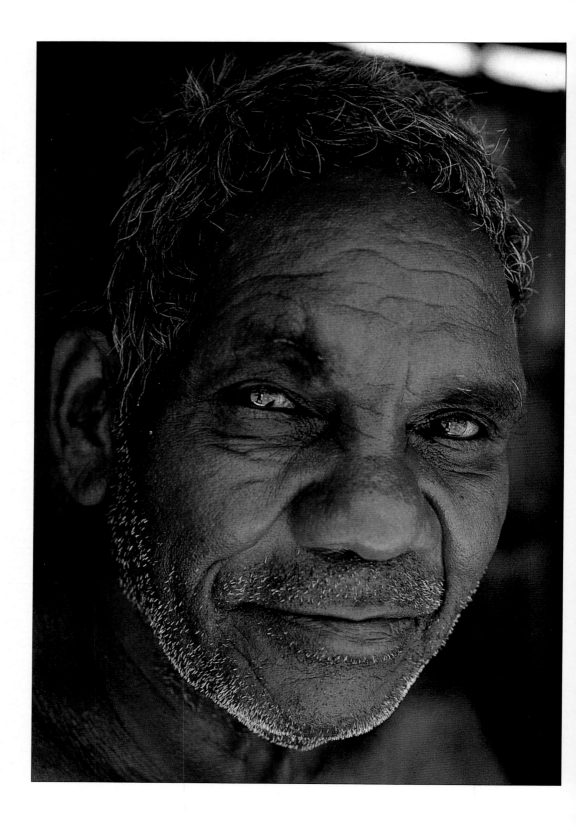

# JACKIE FRIDAY

## YAMBA

At a few minutes before 11 pm on 10 June 1770, the *Endeavour*,
under the command of Lieutenant James Cook, struck a reef north of Cape
Tribulation, off the north coast of Queensland. Cook finally made landfall at
Endeavour River, where he repaired his vessel over a period of two months, during
which time he cultivated amicable relationships with local Aboriginal people,
including the Kuku Yalandji. In his diary Cook noted the presence of a strange
animal, which the local Aboriginal people called 'kanguroo'.

After completing repairs to his ship, Cook was able to sail from the
Endeavour River to continue his exploration north along the coast of Cape York.
The presence of Cook's party is still celebrated by the Kuku Yalandji, who have
traditionally lived in the Daintree Rainforest and along the coastline adjoining
the Great Barrier Reef.

Jackie Friday, who is a senior Kuku Yalandji man, is often called upon to sing the
songs and oversee the ceremonies that ensure the continuance of the Kuku Yalandji
traditions. Today he lives with his family on the Bloomfield River, surrounded by
the tropical rainforest and Kuku Yalandji traditions.

Captain Cook ...
Him first white man we see.
We know him.
He stay with us.

Captain Cook think this good place
Fresh water, plenty of food.
Now everyone come here
Forest [Daintree Rainforest], islands ...
Everyone like this place.

But one thing people forget ...
Don't touch anything.
Ask first.
Captain Cook ...
Him ask first.
But not now
Not any more.

Captain Cook was coming along
He had big anchor,
Big one.
He coming along night time.
Tide going out.
Captain Cook sail right round ...
Into reef.
Tide going out
But him caught on reef.

Him caught till afternoon
Our people watching him
Tide coming in
Him chuck that anchor
But no good.
Anchor ...
He got to leave him.

Captain Cook keep coming along
He come along to beach
He saw our people
He worried
He was going to shoot us.
But Aboriginal people say,
'No, no. We not spear you.
We just want turtle.'
Captain Cook had plenty of turtle there.

He been quieten him up all our people.
He said,
'Alright. I'll keep you close up.
And I'll give you food.'
'What sort?' they said.
'Turtle', he said.
'Good!'

Aboriginal people wanted turtle.
They wanted to try clothes.
Captain Cook said, 'Alright.
I'll give you clothes,
And I'll give you turtle.'

Captain Cook listen to Aboriginal people.
But now everything change ...
Now nobody ask.
Other white people not like Captain Cook.
We got to tell him white people,
Tell him Aboriginal from other place too ...
Not to touch turtle, fish, fresh water.
Don't break our laws ...
If you break our laws ...
Our people die.
But nobody listen now.

*Black Mountain, a significant Aboriginal site
in northern Queensland*

But we can't change our law.
We have to look after our country.
That's the law.

If you cut down tree ...
Any tree,
You get sore.
Then you sick.

Big trees ...
You can't cut him now,
That European law.
But that just new law they make.
Before they want to cut down all of tree,
Just hot place then.

When tree gone,
Animal gone too.
Country change.

Something change with white people
But some stay the same
My grandfather teach me.
Different skin,
But one blood.

Each man from different place.
Different language ...
But same people.

*Monsoon forest*

*Tropical rainforest*

But now white people won't believe us
Because I think he don't like black fella.

I walk around my country.
They say,
'He only black fella
He can't have this place'.

White fella say,
'What you doing here?'
I say, 'I want to build house here,
Want to stay here'.
'No', he say.
'I'll get police.'
And white fella hunt me away.

So I go another place,
Try again.
White man say,
'Hey, what you do here?'

White people come and want to live next to us.
But we don't like that,
Because we know he don't really like us.

Hippie live in rainforest.
He didn't like road [Daintree Rainforest road].
He want that Cape Tribulation for himself.
But that our country.
Hippie say him boss for that country.
They want us sign paper.
But we say 'No'.

We give road for white man.
If flood, big rain,
Then another road alright.
Two roads now.
That good for us too ...
Town closer.

But some places like China Camp,
Nobody can touch.
That big site for us.
That law ...
Aboriginal law.

That China Camp ...
One waterhole in river there.
You can only swim a little bit ...
Must swim slow, not fast.
Can't stir the bottom up ...
Or else it will make big rain,
Big storm.

North Head ...
Can't catch fish there,
Or you'll get sick.
Can't eat fish from there.
One white woman go there,
Before she have baby.
Catch fish and eat it.
Well, that baby been born funny ...
All bent ...
Can't stand up properly.
That baby grow up now.
But still can't stand up properly,
Can't straighten up legs.

Just don't touch anything ...
Ask first.
That's the law.

Maybe people should still be like Captain Cook.
He ask first ...
Look after everything.

We remember Captain Cook.
Still have ceremony for him,
Every year.

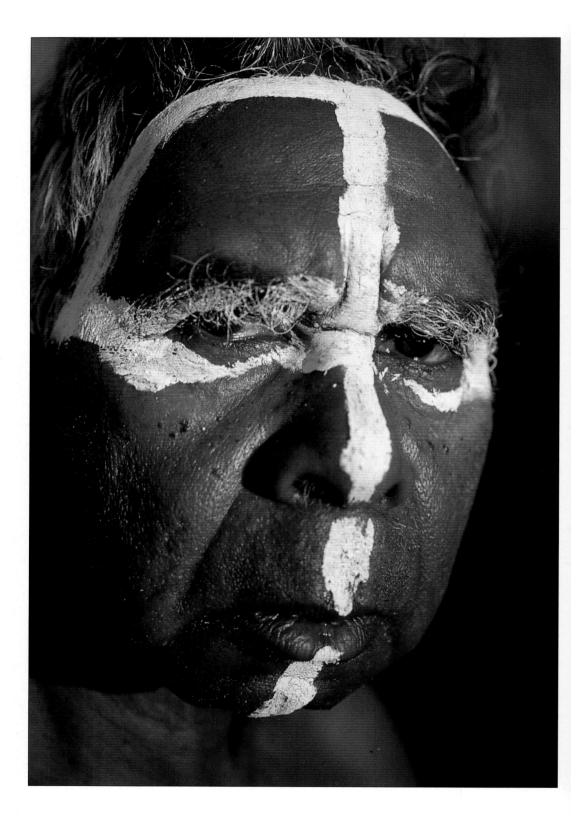

# TOM MURRAY

## DJIMBAWU

Tom Murray was born about 1920. His father and mother had gathered for a large ceremony at a traditional ceremonial ground, on what is now the Ravenshoe Golf Course. While the ceremony was in progress, a fight broke out with a nearby group of pygmy people from Milla Milla.

Before the ceremony had concluded, the police raided the camp, shooting a number of Tom's relatives and forcing the survivors to remain permanently settled in the camp. An influenza outbreak subsequently killed many people in the camp. Tom and his people settled into a working life on the surrounding cattle stations but Tom always maintained his traditional language and culture.

The Djirribal and Girrimayi tribes are generally referred to as the Rainforest People. Among the rainforest groups were the pygmy people, with their characteristic solid wood shields. The Djirribal tribal area encompasses the rainforest surrounding Tully for which Tom still sings the songs.

I was born in Bill Rogers' paddock
My mother and father ...
They came down from Kirrima Station ...
For Buya ceremony.

That was very important business.
Always have that business at same place ...
Ceremony ground.

There was big trouble that time.
Milla Milla people ...
Those pygmy people ...
They came over and there was big fight.
Then police came
They came down and fired shots.
That's the time I was born.
That was about 1920.

That ceremony ground still important for us.
But now it's important place for white people
It's business place for them too.
They call it 'Ravenshoe Golf Course'.

Now everyone says,
'You old man now Tom'.
But not really.

In old days we live to be very old
Eat our own food ...
Bush tucker
No fridge then ...
Everything just fresh.

When we were young,
We couldn't eat everything.
Possum, porcupine, goanna ...
Only for old people.

Old people used to look after the law.
If a man was a real tradesman ...
A lawman,
Then he made dilly bag ...
For ceremony.
You got to pay him for that work,
Pay with cassowary or wallaby.
Maybe you don't pay straight away
But you gotta pay ...
Otherwise he'll come and look for you.

When a law man dies
He won't be buried straight away
Got to be big ceremony for him.
A lawman is very important
Everyone invited to ceremony from all over.

When everybody there
Then there's big talk about that law man ...
Who his mother was ...
Who his father, grandfather ...
Got to think about everything for him.
Then everyone decide who will take over.
Who will be the next law man.

Nobody can touch that body
When he is buried ...
That's the finish.
Can't dig him up.

But if that dead person not a law man ...
Well you got to watch that body ...
That Milla Milla tribe eat people.

If that person died today
They put him in an open grave.
That flesh is fresh.

*Tom and Dolly Murray*

Then tonight couple of fellas take that body ...
Eat flesh.

But a sister can save her brother's body.
Brother and sister is special relationship.
They can't say each other's name
They can't touch each other
They can't eat food that the other has touched.
If a sister steps over her dead brother's body
Then they can't take that body ...
It's not clean any more.

When law men from different tribes meet,
When they talk business together,
Maybe someone might offer you a piece of flesh.
They will tell you who that flesh is from.
They might say ...
'That old so and so.
She that one who ran off with other man.'
Well if you were cranky with that dead person,
You might eat that flesh.

These days people break law all the time.
Like getting married ...
If a married woman break law,
Run off with another man
Then you got to break her neck.
Old days ...
If they married then that's it,
They stay married.
If they run off with someone else
Then they got to die ...
Or get a good belting.

Everybody was scared of pygmy people.
They all know that pygmy people eat flesh
Flesh from dead people.

# TOM MURRAY

But you got to be careful ...
If you talk about other tribes
Then they'll get you.

When head man travels to meeting,
From tablelands down to Ingham
Then he have to camp with head man
from that country where he visit.

When he arrive,
He under guard.
That protect him.
And protect people he's visiting with
Then you give him beef ...
Beef from different humans
Flesh from woman playing up maybe.

That's what we three brothers were
Killer, Collecter, Carrier ...
Me and my two brothers.
One a killer of human being,
One collects the flesh,
Other one carries it down to Ingham.

I should have been the carrier.
But I think I was little bit lucky ...

*Murray Upper, Djirribal country*

White man came ...
Police stopped all that.
I don't think I would have liked to be carrier.
When white people first came
Our people had to fight them.
They clear our country ...
Animals run away,
Bush tucker gone
Only cane ...
Everywhere.

Our old people used to burn cane fields,
Burn around houses.
Then troopers came out to catch us.
But they had gun
So our people gave up fighting.

Police went from camp to camp
They cleaned up ...
Shoot our old people
Kill our kids.

Police sent us all to mission school
Settle us down in one place ...
Civilise us.

Then we had to work for food
We used to slave for nothing,
No holiday.
Work seven days a week.
Little bit of food.
White people just treat us like horse.

If we do anything wrong
Straight to Palm Island.
Police take whole family away.
You don't come back for years.

We not cranky with white people though.
We know we should live together.
But our old people didn't want white people
to come into our country.
That just like when another tribe come,
They come into our country ...
We got to fight.
So our old people got to fight white people.

But white people too strong.
We got to work for them
Work like horses.

Then we lived in humpy
Not in the bush like we should
We just lived around the edge of town.
They settled us on our old ceremony ground ...

Then big sickness came
Nearly everyone died.

That Ravenshoe Golf Course,
Our ceremony ground,
Our people had to camp there ...
And they died there.

That was the biggest ceremony ground
for our culture ...
Then it became our burial ground,
Because so many of our people died from
the sickness.

Now look at where I'm living
This is not even my own country
But now ...
Well, it's hard to change it.

# FELIX HOLMES

## IYANUK

Felix was born around 1905 alongside the tick yard where the bullocks were dipped at Humpty Doo Station near Darwin. As a boy, Felix travelled widely with a droving plant until his initiation ceremony on the western foreshore of Darwin harbour around 1917. At his initiation, Felix was secluded for many weeks, during which time he was instructed in the first parts of the law. His instruction in the law continued at the hands of various senior men over the following years.

After his initiation, Felix returned to droving and at the finish of each muster, he went buffalo shooting across the Alligator River flood plains before returning home to his father's country on the Mary River for Christmas.

During the Second World War, Felix was engaged in stock work with the Australian Army and returned to buffalo shooting after the war.

Felix is the last senior man of the Limilngan tribe. He is responsible for the Mordak mortuary song cycle, which connects the sites and territory of several of the tribes in the Kakadu area with tribes around Darwin.

That was good life that buffalo shooting.
Hard work but always have a good lunch ...
Every day.

After work was finished for the dry season,
Then I walk back to my country.
That way I still know who I am.
I know country, places, songs.

When I sing those songs now
Nobody knows what it is.
When they hear it they say,
'What song is that?'
I tell them that is very important totem song
But they don't know it
They haven't got time to learn it
They say they are too busy
They are too busy with grog
The important things ...
No time for them.

When we have a big ceremony ...
Bury someone,
Young people just come and look at the end.
They come to eat food and grog at the finish.
They don't come to dance or sing.

How can they hang on to the land,
If they don't know the stories or the songs?
They going to lose all their country.

I told them they just rush in for grog.

Now new Aborigines grow up ...
New Aborigines with new totem ...
Grog bottle.

Even if they dance just for tourist ...
That's alright.
Still those young people learning,
And it's good to share with tourists.

Tourist can come to my country.
They can see it for themselves.
See the bush tucker, camping places.
But they got to leave it clean.
Leave it clean like the old times.
That's the law.
That law is for Aboriginal people.
And white people should respect it too.

I don't like to see rubbish on my country.
That's why I got to burn it.
That way I can clean it up.

Even young Aboriginal people make rubbish now.
They drink in pub,
They drink in bush ...
Rubbish everywhere.
Like a pig rooting through the bush.
But, that pig comes from another country.
That's why he behave like that.
He's not from our country.
Doesn't know our law.
But now nuns and church look after our old people.
Well, that good.
But should be job of our young people.

Young people just sit down and watch pensioner.
When pensioner get two or three dollars,
Then younger people chase after them.
That's no good.
They always clean me out.
I'm buggered up then ...

*X-ray rock art, Kakadu National Park, Northern Territory*

No clothes, no food.
When I was young we always look after old people.
That's young people's responsibility.
That's what we teach in ceremonies.
That's our law.

But young people turn away from law.
They never been in Mordak ceremony.
They got no time to learn the law.
If you want to teach young people now ...
Well, you gotta put it on video!

That video is sacred for young people.
They don't know the law,
They don't know the sites.
They just know that video.

I'm only one man.
What can I do?
Just one man.

Young people die from grog,
Too much grog and no tucker.

They don't die from mining,
Just grog.
They just too busy drinking,
Then they die young.

How can we change that?
No respect, no law.
Our people been move around from Koolpinya
to Humpty Doo,
But when we move we lose our country.
If we stay then maybe we got a chance to hang on.
Now we can't even look after the old graves
Because we not allowed to live close by.

*TOP: New cycad growth after fires in a eucalypt forest*

*CENTRE: Water lilies flowering in a dry season billabong*

*BOTTOM: Waterfalls beginning to dry up with the
onset of the dry season*

Young people don't understand.
It was alright to move around in the old days.
Each season you change camp,
But Aborigine not take your country when
you not there.
Now if you move, somebody take your country
before you come back.

Some Aborigines won't go and look after
their country,
They won't leave tourists.
Tourists give them food and money,
But you lose your culture if you stay there.

New Aborigines don't understand ...
They don't know you got to work for country.
They might think about it sometime,
But they never do anything.

You got to work for country ...
Learn ceremonies,
Sing songs,
Visit sites.

When I go back to visit burial ground,
I'm very sad to see new road, building.
Only two lady
Mabel and Flossie
Half-half
They for Vernon Islands and Cape Hotham.
Old Larrakiya man, Mitjilimba ...
Buried other side of creek near Gunn Point
Prison Farm.

Land Councils have to help us keep this culture.
No good to get a lot of money.
If you got no songs or ceremony,

Then you just rich man ...
But you got no story.

Young men just want to sing in band ...
That not right.
That's not for me ...
That's not our culture.
Might be alright if you already know ceremonies
and song,
But these young men don't know our culture.

It's good to live alongside white people,
But I got to keep my culture.
White people ask me about my culture.
I tell them and they listen ...
That's good.

When white people, tourists, ask young people
What young Aboriginal going to say?
When they can't tell white people about culture
White people say, 'This not real Aborigine'.

I'm an old man ...
Just one man.
What can I do?
Hardly any time left.
Aborigine without culture.

I just go away,
Quietly.
Just die in bush ...
Back to my country.

Land Council always got money for meeting.
They got plenty of time for meeting,
Plenty of vehicles for meeting.
But no time for country,

No time for culture,
No time for old people.

Now not much time left.

It's very sad,
Our young people don't care.
Whenever I think about it,
I just have to cry and cry.

When I die ...
It's all finished.
No one knows our law ...
No one cares.
No one even knows where to bury me.

I got to be buried at the South Alligator [River]...
In that big banyan tree,
Right next to the road.
Then after one or two years,
Take my bones and paint them.
Paint them with red ochre first.
Then take them back to Cannon Hill,
Back to Warriyangal ...
In the cave.

Leave my bones at Warriyangal.
Leave them for good ...
Forever.
Then I can see my dreaming from the cave.
That good.

I'll still be sorry for young people,
But I'll be finished ...
And my spirit will look after that dreaming.

# SPLINTER HARRIS

## GULINGA

Splinter's traditional country encompasses the
Northern Territory's Elsey Station, made famous through Jeannie Gunn's book
*We of the Never Never*. Since that time, Splinter's people have been commonly known
as the 'Never Never' people.
The Never Never people are the Mangarray and Yangman tribes.
Unlike most other tribes they have managed to remain on their traditional country
since European contact, mainly by providing the necessary labour for local cattle
stations. Today, the younger men in Splinter's camp still occasionally work the cattle,
while the Never Never people strive to maintain their traditions
through songs and ceremonies.

I'm a Mangarray man.
Mangarray and Yangman tribes ...
We are relations.

This Elsey Station,
Mataranka,
That our country,
All around here.

I been born here.
I been grow up this country.
My father,
My grandfather ...
They taught me this country.

No other person can look to your country
They can't worry for you
When you worry yourself
You gotta worry for your own country.

When we see things happen
Well, we worry
All the time ...
Worry.

These sacred places ...
White man don't know
Only Aboriginal man know
You gotta think that yourself.

Old times ...
Before white people,
When other people come,
They don't know that country.

Argument ...
Big argument
Sometime you gotta do murder

We join together with Djingili,
With Mudburra and Djawoyn
But all other people ...
They gotta go back.

Man might get things from other man's land
In easy time
But dry season ...
Land can't give them nothing there
That land don't know him.

Hodgson Downs Station ...
There's Mangarray and Alawa people
But they only got little block
And fence all around it.
Land not made for fence
Fence cut off land ...
Cut off life,
That wire will strangle man.

Not like us,
We go wherever we want ...
Darwin, Alice Springs, Queensland
We're free.

On Elsey Station we go anywhere.
Station manager good people.
They use the land right.
They not change the country.
Country still comes back each year.

When it rains ...
Trees grow,
Grass grow,
That country comes back.

We got everything for this country
We still got song

*Splinter Harris at Djembray*

*Vegetation fringing the freshwater rivers often yields
freshwater mussels*

We got story
We got ceremonies ...
Everything still here.

Old people teaching,
And young people listen.
They know the rules,
They must listen.

If they don't listen,
They get it hard way.
We send them away to the bush ...
For hard ceremony.

That ceremony ...
Punishment ceremony.
Young people gotta stay.
They not allowed to come out.

Couple of big men there,
They're policemen.
They keep boys there,
Make 'em stay hard way.

When ceremony finished ...
Those boys come back.
They real good then ...
No humbug.

No arguments any more
They don't make fight,
Carry wood for old people,
Get water when you ask him,
Real quiet then.

We are Yangman tribe,
Yangman and Mangarray.

*Wet season growth*

We live together ...
One people.
Never Never people.

All this country ...
From King River,
Right through Mataranka,
All the way to Warlock.
Top side from Mountain Valley,
Bottom side Gorrie and Nutwood Downs.
All one country ...
We all one people.

White people come,
Bring cattle.
They build homestead.
But little bit later,
They leave.

Next mob come along,
More cattle.
New homestead.
But they leave too.

All the time new people.

Nat Buchanan
He brought cattle first time
Long time ago
He come along through our country
Bring cattle from Queensland.

First Glenco Station,
Then Springvale
Close up to Katherine
Then Elsey Station.

*The last of the wet season sunsets, signalling the onset*
*of an early dry season*

Mr Gunn come along after that
First time him just manager
Then he brought his missus
That little missus we call her ...
Mrs Gunn.

Our old people were here
They worked for Mr Gunn.

My old father ...
Jack Wulinjawon,
He used to work for Mr Gunn.
Here on Elsey Station.

All our old people work here,
Right from the start,
Cutting timber,
And build that homestead.

Then we been work there ...
Stockwork,
Mustering,
Everything.

Old Elsey Dick,
Old Nim Galpudu,
Jawolgin,
Kakalay ...
All Mangarray men,
Working on Elsey Station.

When old Mr Gunn finished at Elsey [died],
They carried all that iron to new station
But that still our country ...
Yangman and Mangarray ...
All mixed
So our people did that work.

Man can't work somebody else's country ...
Only his own.

They all done now ...
Mr Gunn,
Old stockmen.
They all finished ...
But still there,
Buried.
All buried on Elsey.

We still look after our country,
Yangman and Mangarray tribes.
We share it with white people.
We made Conservation Park.
But we never forget our old people,
White people and Aboriginal ...
Together.

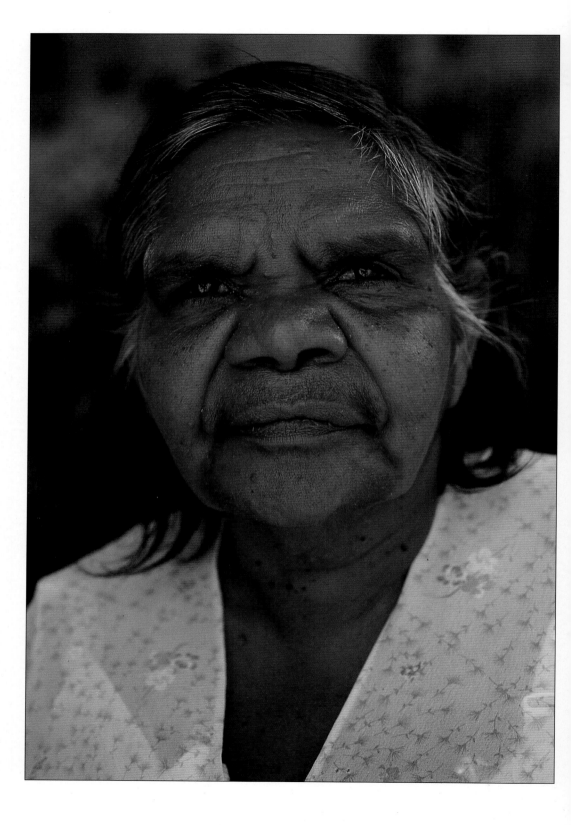

# EILEEN BELIA

Unlike many other Aboriginal people, Eileen was able to remain
on or close by her traditional tribal country as she grew up. She was taken from the
camp as a young girl and brought into the homestead to work in 'the big house'. Later,
she worked on many other stations in Western Queensland, unlike many of her family
who were forcibly removed to Queensland's infamous Palm Island, losing touch
with their family, country and traditions.
Eileen now lives in a small outback town in Western Queensland, maintaining contact
with her country and traditions and providing a focus for many of her kinsfolk who
want to maintain their heritage.

51

First I got to tell you about my grandfather.
Kaitjindu,
That's his name,
My mother's father.
He was Belangu tribe.

My father ...
He was Waluwarra tribe
His father was a Waluwarra,
And also his grandfather.

I'm come from two groups ...
Waluwarra and Belangu.

I was born on the Barkly,
In a little creek,
Near Barkly Homestead
During a big ceremony.

Everyone was there for the ceremony,
Waluwarra, Belangu, Yirringa, Wakaya tribes ...
All the tribes were there,
All mixed together.

But us mob,
When we finished there
We come back down to Headingly Station,
To our camp ...
Belangu camp.
Big camp there.

We lived there for years and years,
My father,
My grandfather,
My great grandfather,
Belangu and Waluwarra tribes ...
We lived together there.

I was born there,
Must have been in the 1920s.
Probably late 1920s I reckon.
I'm not sure but something around then.

My father and mother travelled.
They used to go all over to ceremonies
Over to Barkly,
Down the Georgina River to Roxborough Station,
That's where the main camp was.
We were really Georgina River people.

When my father took his wife,
That's the time he worked on the station,
He used to work from Headingly [Station]
He was drover.
Later when I come along,
We used to travel with him.

When we was travelling,
We all had horses.
We kids had our own horses.
They were all station horses.

At Christmas time we had holidays.
That's when we had ceremonies.
We travelled all around to ceremonies.
Travelled in our own buggy.
We had our own buggy and horses then.

While we were travelling,
We used to put our swags in the buggy.
Then walk on to visit the camps,
See all our relatives and friends.

The main camp was near Lake Nash.
Eighteen miles this side of Lake Nash.

*Eileen Belia*

We travel from Headingly to the eighteen mile camp.
That was the main camp.
Lots of Aboriginal people there,
All tribes.

From Lake Nash we travelled on ...
We went to Beantree,
That's another big camp.
Then on to Barkly.

We used to have our own corroborees,
Just our ones.
No other tribe would dance there ...
At Urandangi there
Only for Waluwarra that one.

When I was growing up,
I worked on the stations too.
I worked on Headingly, Rocklands,
Avon, Hoven, Carandotta.
I had a housemaid's job.

I didn't miss out on anything.
I still went to ceremonies and everything.
Whenever there was a ceremony,
Well they used to take me down there.

The policeman took us away to work.
We were about twelve years old then.
That policeman was really strict.
If we didn't go to work,
We got sent to Palm Island.
'Send you away from your parents', he'd tell us.
If our parents tried to stop him,
Then they got sent to Wurabinda Mission.
Grown-ups got sent to Wurabinda,
And children got sent to Palm Island.

*Spinifex in the southern part of Waluwarra country, western Queensland*

One time old Fred and Dora Age got sent away.
They tried to stick up for their rights ...
But they got sent away.
Dora was real fair skin,
And policeman said it wasn't right ...
Can't have light woman living in blackfella's camp.
Fred and Dora stuck up for their rights,
So they got sent away.

We never had no schooling.
We weren't allowed to go to school.
They just took us away to work ...
When we was twelve years old.

Headingly Station was my first job.
I stayed there a good while.
When the manager went away,
I went back to camp.

But that policeman used to check us up.
He'd come round the camp.
'Eileen Age ...
Where's that girl?'

Well I got so as I'd look for work myself.
I'd go out after Christmas,
Leave my family,
And look for work.

I was lucky
Nearly every station I work for
They was good people.
They would feed me, clothe me,
And take me to town ...
Mount Isa, Cloncurry, Townsville.
I used to get around with them.
But sometimes I said 'No,
I got to get back for ceremony'.
So they used to take me back,
Then pick me up when it was over.

There was old Morton, Shaler, Smith.
Mrs Smith was on Carandotta
She was a good lady.
Old Morton was a German ...
He was on Headingly Station.

Crowly was on Obon Station.
Alan Jack and Sue Jack from Rocklea Station.
They was nice people them two.
They never slinging off at dark people.

The Mortons used to take us down the corroboree.
They used to stay right through.
Then they go home late.
I had my own room in the main house.
They say,
'The door will be open when you get home'.
Then I'd stay for the rest of the corroboree ...
We had to stay till morning.

When I was on Carandotta
I was working for Smiths.
I was the baby-sitter for the two small kids.
I used to wash them, feed them,
Clean them, put them to bed.

Mortons used to have a buggy.
He used to come into Urandangi ...
Come from Headingly for groceries.

Smiths got a car.
We travelled all the way to Townsville,
And they took me with them.
They took me everywhere with them.

All the way along we just camp out each night.
We each had a big swag.
He was a real bushman Mr Smith.
He'd just chop a tree down and make a windbreak,
Make tea in a billy can.

It took us four nights along the road.
We had a flat tyre on that plain,
Down near Hughenden somewhere there ...
Lot of timber there.
Mr Smith would say,
'We coming to that big plain now'.
So the kids would gather up the wood,

*Initially, the Waluwarra people competed with the cattle for water. Later, the pastoralists became dependent on the Waluwarra as stockmen.*

Chuck it on the back,
On the trailer.
There'd be plenty of firewood for later then.

I found a goanna ...
Caught him and cooked him.
The Smiths ate him alright.
We stopped at that river,
Everyone went off to the toilet.
One of the kids yelled out
'Big goanna'.
Well they all off and into it.
We got him and cooked him.
They got into that tail.

Smiths saw me get that goanna fat ...
I greased my foot with it you know.
It's like rubbing yourself with Vaseline ...
Stops your feet from cracking.

You use emu fat like that too.
That good for colds too that emu fat.
You can use that fat on your saddle too.
Mr Smith asked me what I was doing.
I told him.

Goanna fat and eucalyptus ...
That's the best medicine.
Rub your chest with that.
It's a bit hard to get emu fat now.

You can't keep emu fat in a jar ...
I tried it in a honey jar once.
Not in jar, not a tin.
That emu fat just goes straight through.
If you put it in at night,
Next morning it'll be empty.

Well one time they took me to the pictures.
There was a big heap of sand,
And we all sat on that.
They had a cowboy picture ...
That was my first time.

Those cowboys were shootin',
And we was ducking behind each other.
Well we said,
'We got to get out of here or we'll get shot'.
So we grabbed the blanket we was sittin' on
And ran off.

I was living in the same house with the Smiths,
Down there in Townsville.
They bought me new clothes,
Shoes and socks.
I was dressed up like a white kid,
All flashed up.

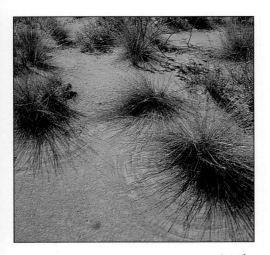

*Spinifex*

I looked at the sea,
That big stretch of blue water.
'How far does that go?' I kept asking.

The Smiths was going over to Palm Island,
But I wouldn't get in the boat.
I stayed home.
I was frightened for that blue water,
But I was more frightened of Palm Island.
All that blue water round it,
No way of gettin' back to your family.
We always been told about Palm Island.
If we didn't go to work,
Then we gunna be sent to Palm Island ...
In the middle of the blue water ...
In the middle of the sea,
And no way of coming back.

Well they already had some of our people.
They took them away to there.
So I was too frightened to go there.

The Smiths went to Palm Island,
Just for one day.
Then they came back.
But I wouldn't go,
No way.

Just after that they was bombing Darwin.
That German manager, Old Morton from
Headingly,
He had to leave
But I don't know why.

Old Cowboy and Woodcutter,
They used to work for Old Morton.
That Slippery, Frank and Banjo at Amaroo Station ...

They're called Morton cause they worked there.
They had no 'nother name before,
And he was good to them.

Same as my grandfather,
My father's father,
He worked for old Mr Age on Walgara.
So he took that name.
Before that he just had his straight out name,
And we kept that name on.

In those days young people was different ...
The boys was in the single men's camp,
And the girls stayed with the old women.
That way they didn't mix together.
Only married people were together.
Young people weren't allowed to drink.
Old people used to give them a belting.

Them days young people were different ...
They had respect for old people.
But maybe if we started up the ceremonies ...
Maybe they might change.
Maybe they might learn the corroboree.

My grandfather had the last corroboree.
That was at Urandangi.

I used to talk to my grandfather,
Talk about our country,
Our background ...
Whole lot of things.

Well one time
There was me and my two aunty,
Tibby and Rosie.
They were young then,
They didn't have no one [not married].

Rosie went to work at Hoven then
Tibby stayed on at Headingly.

Well, these two blackfellas come down drovin'.
They used to come down every year
They came down for race meeting this time
They was Pitjantjara men them two.
Anyway they come to Hoven this time.

Then while they there one night,
Rosie goes walking around down the dump.
Well she must 'ave been expecting them people eh?
And they took off with her.
From there they dressed in Kadaitja clothes.

Well everyone was looking for her.
She'd been missin' all night ...
All the next day.
So they tracked her,
Followed her track.

*Sunset over the Georgina River, near Camooweal*

*The dry season across Waluwarra country*

Well that track came towards Carandotta,
There's another little place there,
Beanla ...
A little camp there with a lot of people.

Well old Left Hand and Shorty
They got on to them two,
They was working some stations
So they got them two to track her.

They had old Joe Patterson
He was an old blackfella ...
A tracker from Mount Isa
He was a Kalkadoon [tribe] that old fella
That was Henry Kitchener's mother's father see?

Alright,
They track them.
They seen that track
Seen where it went to this tree.
And they seen the clothes there ...
Hanging up in this tree.

Well they must have put her in the other clothes ...
Kadaitja clothes.
From there that footprint left that tree ...
You think they could see it!

Well she must have been know something.
She know her two son been looking for her,
Because her toe mark there.
She just move her foot in that Kadaitja shoe
And she left toe mark for her two son.

Well that policeman from Urandangi,
He couldn't see no track.
'They must have killed her', he said.

63

But they could hear this bird sing.
Well, old people used to tell us that devil bird.

They follow that bird and climb a tree.
They could see something moving.
Well she just show herself to her two son.
She said, 'Sons, don't follow me.
I'm with the two travelling blackfellas.'
They couldn't really see her.
But they could hear her.

Well their hair started to stand up.
So they said to the policeman,
'We'll never find her no more,
She's gone.
She could end up in Alice Springs or anywhere.'

Couple of years later I was staying with Tibby ...
Over on Carandotta.
Well that woman showed up that night.
All that came in was a ball of string.
Aunty Tibby said,
'Don't touch it'.
So we never touched it.
I just jumped straight up on the bed.
Then they come to this old cook.
They said,
'You know where my daughter and grand-daughter is?'
He said, 'Yeah, they over there in the hut'.
So we shifted up into the main house then.

We told the manager what happened
And he understand.
They was Gibsons, the managers,
And they come round Alice Springs
So they know about these Kadaitja men.

Alright,
Two years after
We find out she's at Alice Springs ...
With those two blokes.

She was Jessie Kitchener.
Maybe she got family by them blokes now.
Jessie Katjundi, Jessie Kitchener,
She was my grandmother.

Cecil Moonlight,
He's Wangkungurru tribe,
He saw her there.

My grandmother ...
My mother's mother
She not really belong to this country
She met my grandfather down Cluny Station.
He picked her up while he was droving.

When we had ceremony
Each tribe camp by themselves
We all have big corroboree at Urandangi
But each tribe got to be coaxed
If they don't come in for their dance ...
Then big trouble.

Belangu and Waluwarra tribes,
They were close together.
My grandfather and great grandfather,
They were the big men for those tribes.

My father lived in the big camp.
That big camp at Headingly.
Well they had the same thing at Urandangi,
And they brought us into town.
But we only come in for race meetings or Christmas.

*Drought in western Queensland*

We do our twelve months on the station.
Not allowed to go away during that time,
Then come into town at Christmas ...
Only once a year.

We used to get tucker and clothes,
And a few bob too.
The postman used to give us our money,
But the police used to take that ...
We just blackfellas.

That time white fellas not allowed near blackfellas,
And blackfella not allowed to drink in the pub.
We was under the Act then.
But some station managers were good.
We used to eat in the kitchen with them.
Hoven and Carandotta Stations were good.
But Glenormiston ...
Oh ... that manager was no good.
The dark boys ate out at the wood heap.

They used to put their tucker in a big dish,
And have a big billy can of tea.
No cups, no spoon,
Just all dip their bread in.

Them days you not even allowed to get your money.
The policeman keep your money.
But when you go to get it,
You only allowed to have a little.
No matter you been saving it,
You only allowed to get maybe ten pounds.

Then when the Act finished,
Well it all change then.
One white man come along,
He said, 'How you get your money?'
We told him.
Then he gave us a little pocket book each.
After that we always take our pocket book.
Then we can check up how much we got.

Then we see that some of us got a lot of money.
Well that's good then.
One fella even got enough to buy a car.

We weren't allowed into town.
Police used to chase us back down the river.
We weren't allowed to go to Mount Isa,
Same for all the working men.
Straight back to Urandangi.
'Get back down the river',
That's what they used to tell us.
We only allowed to leave for holidays,
Just one week before Christmas.
Then got to be back,
One week after New Year.

I got married when I was on Carandotta.
I was working for Crowleys then.
Crowleys took it over after Smith went.
Johnny Belia was working there then
When I married Johnny we stay together then.

Later, when we had kids we moved to Dajarra ...
We wanted the kids to have some schooling.
Johnny used to travel back and forth to the stations,
But I stayed on in Dajarra.

That lasted about ten years,
Then we split up.
Now he lives next door ...
He's pensioned off now.

But when I was a kid,
We had a good time before we start work.
It different now.

We free now.
But ceremonies all finished ...
No one following up now.
Only old Dubbo Rose and Percy Age.
Percy, that Fred Age's son,
They the only two that can sing now.

Quartpot,
George Quartpot ...
He's singing corroboree all the time.
He's always at it.
He talk Yirringa lingo.

Young people don't know it.
They haven't got the time to learn.
The old ways are just about gone.

Soon the Waluwarra will be finished.
Only my brother Johnny Age and me now,
That's all.

All Belangu gone now.
Soon Waluwarra will be gone too.
We only got one more chance.
We have to get the young people together,
Then we got to tell them ...
Tell them how important this is.
Teach them the stories and songs.

I'm moving back to Urandangi soon.
Then my brother Johnny and me,
We can start with them young people
Percy can speak Belangu language,
So he can help too.

When you gettin' old, well ...
You gotta leave a good story.
We just a few left now.
Me, Johnny Age and Jessie ...
We gotta get that story together.
We should just slip out into the bush ...
Take some young people and teach 'em.

I reckon I'm gonna try.

# MICK WAGU

## WAGU

Mick grew up in Central Australia where he worked mainly
as a stockman. He was initiated into the traditions of his tribe and began a lifetime
of learning the law.

After many years of stock work, Mick got his own droving plant together with the help
of his friend, Bryan Bowman, a European station owner. The many droving trips
through the arid regions of Central Australia finally afflicted Mick with sandy blight
and blinded him. This brought his droving days to an end but did not diminish
his status as an Aboriginal law man.

Today Mick lives at Mbangara outstation on Nawietooma Station. He is widely known
and respected in Central Australia as a law man and is particularly responsible for the
Native Cat song cycle.

I was born in Arranda country ...
Place called Arrampiri.
That's on Glen Helen [Station].
Don't know what year that was [around 1920],
But old Charlie Myers was at Haast's Bluff then.
He was holding horses on agistment.
He had a lot of sheep, cattle and goats.

Old Charlie used to say,
'If you don't round those horses up,
you lousy bugger,
I won't bring back no lollie from Alice Springs'.

He just give us shirt,
No trousers.
He was funny old man.

Old Charlie used to have a shed at Ulumbarr ...
Haast's Bluff Spring.
Three men got killed there ...
Murdered.
So old Charlie moved from there.

Those dead men were Luritja tribe.
Their own family murdered them ...
When they had a ceremony, well ...
Those three men were swearing.
Swearing in the ceremony.
Well, that was it.

That family killed them at the ceremony.
Those old men couldn't stand that swearing.
Nearly one hundred people there,
Then big fight before sunrise.
When sun get up that morning,
Those three men dead.

# MICK WAGU

Old Kangaroo Jim's grandfather,
Wintjirrkiri,
His mother's father ...
He got killed.
He was really Luritja tribe.
But little bit Arranda because ...
Well, he used to live with them Arranda,
Down in Bullocky Creek.
That's the border for Arranda.

Old Kuniya got killed too.
He was Luritja tribe too.
He was old Tom Ukinyi's younger brother.
Old Fred Raggett used to call him Larrikin Tom
'Cause he was always chasin' women ...
Other men's wives.

Putaya was the other one killed ...
Speared him right through ...
Dead.
Early in the morning,
Straight off.

Brawn Raggett's father ...
He was made young man at that ceremony
[initiated].

My father was old Kulay ...
Half Warlpiri,
Half Luritja ...
Warlpiri-Ngaliya.

My father grew me up ...
Halfway up,
Then I worked for white men ...
Worked for old Fred Raggett,
Down at Glen Helen.

*Kangaroo Jim, Mick Wagu's mate*

Worked there right through until I was a man,
Then I became a bush man ...
One full year.

After that I worked at Hamilton Downs ...
Stock work.
Me and Frank Poepel work there,
For Ted Harris.
Me and Frank done all that yard,
That old station at Hamilton Downs,
I done one full year there.

Then I worked for old Ted.
He got me to bring one racehorse to Alice.
Me and old Jim Impu,
We brought him down.
Camped one full night on the way.

Old Jim said,
'I got a job up Top End,
Can you join me?'
So I did.
We went to Frew River Station.

We saw the boss ...
Arthur Henley,
He was the owner for Frew River Station.
The manager came along to look for us,
But we already waiting for him.
That Frank Bottler was the manager.
He saw us two ...
And he had dinner with us.
Then he pick one man,
That Alyawarra man [Alyawarra tribe]
To get plant [droving plant].

*Mick Wagu and family at Mbangara outstation*

Next night,
We moved to another waterhole ...
Mustering horses.
Just me, Jim and one young Pintupi fella.
We mustered right down to Tea Tree waterhole,
Camp there.
Then drove them horses to Frew River Station.
About one hundred head of horses we had.

We were mustering,
Branding all the cattle.
We stopped there one year,
Had one Christmas there.

Boss gave us plant of horses ...
Two pack horses and one riding horse each.
That Christmas ...
We brought that plant of horses to Hatches Creek.

But after one year ...
I argue with that boss.
That gear in the packs ...
It was broken,
But I didn't tell the boss for long time.
He was cranky with me,
'That strap was broken.
Why didn't you tell me?
Now all the gear smashed.
You was boss of the plant.'

Then I strike out ...
Went west.
I carried my swag on my back.

While we worked for him,
He paid us ten shillings a week.
Another ten shillings we spent on clothes.

Five shillings for one shirt,
Boss supplied tucker and swag.

That was before the war.

I walked back to Hatches Creek
Got a job on Wolfram mining,
Five shillings a week.
I worked there for another year.

My job was drilling,
Down in the drive.
There weren't much light ...
We only had a candle.
The boss sent us away one Christmas
He say,
'Everyone have a holiday,
But come back after Christmas'.
I say,
'Oh good. I'll be back.'
But when we gone I say,
'Bugger that,
Five shillings a week.
Too much hard work.'

I travelled to Jay Creek,
And saw Johnny McCormack there.
He brought a camel train down through Jay Creek.
Old Johnny wanted to go to Alice for Christmas,
So I joined him.
We had Christmas in Alice that year.

I saw one man in Alice ...
Albert Morris.
He come along to pick up racehorses.
Take 'em to Hamilton Downs.
I joined him to drove those racehorses back.

*Many stories of Central Australia tell of the formation of outstanding geographic features, such as these ranges, and thus link many tribes in their ritual life*

I stayed at Hamilton Downs for a few years,
Working for ten shillings a week.

Old Tom Makarinya,
That Arranda man ...
He was living there then.
Old people were still there.

Anyway,
I was working there.
And old time
He show me all them sacred sites.
Charlie Snake,
Tom's brother,
He took me round for sacred places too.

# MICK WAGU

*Mick Wagu*

Arranda and Luritja
Both used to live in Bullocky Creek,
Dashwood Creek too.
That's the boundary there,
For Arranda and Luritja.
That's why I can live at Mbangara.
I finished up at Hamilton Downs,
Then I went back to Glen Helen.
I been finished all that work ...
Frew River, Hatches Creek, Hamilton Downs.
I stayed at Glen Helen then.

I worked with Bryan Bowman at Glen Helen,
Stock work, droving, working with camels.

Bryan give me job ...
Cartin' flour with twelve camel team,
From Alice to Glen Helen.

Camels good to work with.
You can't camp for lunch ...
No dinner camp,
Only supper you stop.
Make big supper camp.

Every night got to hobble camels.
When they get perishin' for water,
Those camels be gone.
Two days no water for camel,
Loaded up with heavy load ...
Poor bugger.

One time we went from Glen Helen
to Hermannsburg,
Pick up big charcoal engine.
We had big bull camel with that team.

We got to take engine to Raggett Well,
But that bull not strong enough to carry engine.

We load engine on that bull camel ...
It nearly flatten him ...
He couldn't get up.
No good.

So we took another load to Glen Helen ...
Two inch pipe and trough.
We saw big fat camel,
Wild one.
We took it back to Hermannsburg.
It was bigger than that bull.

We got it to Hermannsburg.
That big fat camel got up that engine ...
No trouble.
Took it all the way to Raggett's Well,
That's Glen Helen.
Glen Helen is really Raggett's Well
Proper name.

That rail come to Oodnadatta [railway line],
Finish there.
Camels bring gear from Oodnadatta to Alice.
Then other teams take over,
Take it on to other stations.

Old Wallace Foggaty,
He had a big shop on west side from river.
Camels bring them stores from Oodnadatta.
Then those old Afghans pick them up,
Take them to other stations ...
And all up the line too [telegraph line].

I was carting wool for Bryan Bowman.
He had 500 or 1000 sheep,

That's when I learnt to shear.
We only had hand shears.
Then we cart the wool on camels to Alice.

Later Bryan Bowman give me job on stock work,
Bringing station plant into Alice Springs.
Then Bryan changed his mind ...
He make Tom Raggett boss for that plant.
Then we drove two mobs into Alice.
From Alice they trucked them south.

Then Bryan bought Conniston Station.
We worked both sides then,
Did that for years and years.

Old Bryan bought a truck then
So I learnt to drive him.
Then Bryan help me buy my own truck.
It cost 300 pounds.
Then I could do contract work.

Old Bryan was good man ...
He trust me.
I like old Bryan.
When my motor car broke ...
Old Bryan help me.
We live together.

After that we went to Mount Wedge ...
Bill Woodby's place.
When the drought was on,
We moved cattle to there.
I took a tank over to Labara Bore.
Bryan drove the cattle over.
I took the tank on my truck
And me and Bryan put the tank up.

Then I drove cattle for Bryan.
I took a mob to Alice.
Bryan gave me a saddle, bridle and packhorse.
I asked him to help me get a brand,
From that stock inspector,
Just a brand for my horses.

Well I got that brand ...
'M.I.T.'
Then I used to get brumbies,
Catch them in a trap yard.
Half for Bryan ...
Half for me.

Then I had my own plant.
Used to bring cattle and get paid.
I got thirty shillings for each bullock.

*Senior women are custodians of the important*
*women's ceremonies of the Luritja*

# MICK WAGU

*Many dreamings for the Luritja traditions pass through Haast's Bluff*

I drove them to the trucking yards,
And they shipped them to Adelaide.

I did that for about six years.
I have five boys working for me ...
Ten pounds per week while we were droving.
I used to buy tucker for the boys.
We bought a 'killer' for on the road.
Bryan was a really fair man,
He would give us one dry cow for the road.

One really dry Christmas,
Really hot days,
I was droving a mob of 300 cows
From Conniston to Anbala Station.
It was a private contract.
I was droving up at the back of the mob.
It was hot and dry.
The wind was blowing dust back at me ...
Dust in my eyes for the whole trip.

When I got to Anbala,
I could only see a little bit.

We got paid in Alice Springs by Brian Muldoon.
He was the stock and station agent.
I could see a little bit to walk around.
I paid all my boys,
And went back to Anbala Station.

I saw old Mort Conway at Anbala.
He was a taxi man at that time.
I asked old Mort to bring a drum of petrol for me,
Then pick me up at Anbala.

Mort brought the petrol and picked me up.
Then he took me and the petrol to Glen Helen.

Old Mort ...
He's the best man out of the whole lot.
He knows just about all the native law.

I stopped at Glen Helen for a month
My left eye was already buggered up ...
From the early days.
Then that dust finished me off ...
Blind.

Bryan paid for me to go to Adelaide ...
For the operation.
I stopped at Adelaide for three months.
I came home then,
I was worried for my family.
My eyes got worse.
The cornea graft didn't fix it.
Doctor said I should have stopped longer,
Another month in Adelaide he said.

I done wrong myself,
And now I'm blind.
These days it's different.
They can send family down with you.
But not then.

Now I sit down at Mbangara,
On Dashwood Creek.
I look after the law,
But it's very hard ...
These young men won't listen.
They're all the time silly with grog.
If you want a drink,
You only need a couple of drinks.

They don't know nothing ...
Nothing about family,
Nothing about law.

Young people don't obey law,
Not Aboriginal law,
Not white law.
You have to get police.

In the next few years,
Everything is going to be properly wrong.

My wife died a couple of years ago,
I'm very sorry for that.
One of my daughters died too.

I'm a law man ...
I look after the law.
I've got the responsibility ...
But I haven't got a son.

# PADDY ROE

## DJAGAN

Paddy Roe was born around 1912 on Roebuck Plains Station near
Broome in Western Australia. Quickly abandoned by his European father, Paddy was
sought by police as part of a policy to remove coloured children from their Aboriginal
families. He was hidden from authorities by his mother and sent out into the desert,
where he learnt the law under the charge of his uncles. As an adult, no longer fearing
removal by police, Paddy returned to his birth place and took a wife, but the
elopement eventually brought the wrath of Aboriginal law upon Paddy.
Paddy now lives in Broome and is widely respected as the 'old man'
who maintains the Bugarrigarra — the dreaming and the law — he learnt
from the old people.

I'm Nyekini tribe
Same as my Aboriginal father
Dampier Downs is Nyekini country
All the way to Noonkanba
That's where we met Walmatjarri people.

I was born on Roebuck Plains Station
Near Sheep Camp bore
That's Yawuru ...
Country for Yawuru tribe.

Old George Roe
He was station manager then
My mother was working for him
She was station cook.

Those times were different
White man could take anything
If he like Aboriginal woman
He just take her
That way I was born
Just for tea and sugar.

But George Roe left me then
Put me back into the camp
He didn't want to know me
But my Aboriginal father
Old Bullu
He took me
He start to grow me up.

Little bit later
Policeman come along
He looking for children
Half caste kids
He pick 'em up
Just like lambs
Never been ask.

When mothers and fathers complain
Policeman just knock 'em down
Flog them with a chain.

My mother seen this happen
So she send me away
Back into the bush
Past Dampier Downs
Out into the desert.

I stayed out there for long time
With my mother's young sister
We living off the land
First thing I learnt was hunting
My uncles teach me everything.

Old Bullu, my father
He died while I was away
My mother's sister and her husband
They looking after me
And then I learnt the law.

When I was a man
I came back to Roebuck Plains
And I heard a story ...
About one old man in the desert.

He had three wives
Some men wanted those women
So they killed him
Just to get the women
One of these women
The young one
She was brought to Roebuck Plain.

Well I was watching her
I was keeping an eye on her,
Just thinking.

# PADDY ROE

*Paddy Roe*

One day she come to me and say,
'We should run away together'.
She don't want no old man
She was still young ...
Like me.

Well we run away
Right up to Broome,
They couldn't find my track
Because I didn't walk on dirt
Just step on grass.
That was about 1928.

That's where I meet Mr Douglas
Him and Mrs Douglas
They just starting up here
Try to make a farm.

Well I went up to see Mr Douglas
Left my woman in the bush
I told Douglas that I run away
So he give me job
And nobody knew I was there.

I lived with the old people then
They were Djugun tribe
No young people left
Only about sixty old people.

These old people told me about their country,
They taught me the lot
All this country ...
Never missed an inch.

I said to my old wife,
'I think these people are mad
I think they gonna kill me.
I'm a stranger here.'

# PADDY ROE

*Build-up to the wet season storms over Nyekini country*

We were sitting down on the beach
Made a camp there,
I ask them old people,
'What for you fella tell me story,
Story for all this country,
Take me and camp all over,
Tell me for this country?'

Well, these old women stand up,
'Oh', they said.
'Can't you understand?'
'You see us old women? ...
Sisters?
Where our men?
There, sitting over there.'

'Well we are old people and
We can't have no babies.
You got young wife
And you'll have plenty of children?'

All these old people died ...
1933 last one died.
They had daughters
But they went to different countries
Philippine,
Chinese,
Japanese,
Kupang.
Some white fellas too.
They take all these daughters
And never come back.

Well I'm the only one left.
I stayed on this country
I know every little inch
Never miss one part.
That's how I get this country.

But later on I had to go back
I have to give myself up
If you take women ...
That alright.
But you gotta go back,
Face these people,
That's the law.
Mr Douglas was very sad.
He was sorry to see us go.

We walk all along the beach.
Below the water line ...
No one can track us then.
We walk for two weeks.

I sent message ahead,
'I'll be coming back' ...
They knew what for.
They were waiting what for me.

Just before sunrise
I come up to that fighting ground.
They were all there ...
Waiting for me.

I only got shield ...
No boomerang,
No spear.
I give up myself to these people.

At six o'clock, sunrise they start.
They throwing boomerang,
All through morning,
Right up to lunch time.

My mothers-in-law
They held the spears
They break them
Before man can spear me in the leg
Mother-in-law break them.
They can do that
They save me
That's the law.
Not one spear get me,
Not one boomerang,
I never get one mark.

Then last man coming in
Just about sundown
I can hardly see him
I was so tired.

*The coastline is still a traditional source of food for Paddy Roe and his family, following the old ways of the Nyekini people*

That first boomerang
He got me in the leg
Boomerang broke off
And stick in my leg.

He know he got me that man
So he come to me
And give me spear
'Here, you spear me', he said.
'No', I said.
'I done something wrong
So I can't spear you.'
I got to get punished.

He done the right thing
He get me with boomerang
So he give me chance to spear him.
But I was wrong
So I say 'No'.

# PADDY ROE

Then it was finished.

No motor car then
So they get wheelbarrow
And push me to hospital
So I still got that mark
Right here on my knee.

Then that woman was mine
My wife
And that who my children from.
Proper way
Aboriginal way.
Follow the law.

Now I'm teaching me kids
I saw a long way behind

*Dry season sunset on the tropical Western Australian coast*

And I see a long way in front
So I've been thinking
Hanging on to law.

We still got Aboriginal law
Bugarrigarra we call it
We sing songs for it
But not like guitar
Guitar you can make song
Sing that song anywhere.

But Aboriginal song
No good for other country
Only for one area ...
One country one song
That's Aboriginal law.

This guitar business is very strange to me
All the time new songs
Make one song ...
Chuck him away
Make another one
Chuck him away too
All the time new one coming up.
But Aboriginal law ...
It always stay the same.

Broome,
This is Djugun country
But they are finished
No one left alive.

I look after this country
I'm Nyekini
I speak Nyekini language
But I'm looking after Djugun.

I'm a Nyekini man,
Born on Yawuru country
Living on Djugun land
But I can't hang on by myself.
So I've been thinking
Thinking of new way
Which way we gotta go now.

I used to camp behind tree
White man camp behind another tree
I look from behind my tree ...
He hide
He look from behind his tree ...
I hide.

I thinking ...
Got to cut down tree and see each other properly.

We should sit down together.

We don't have to live in each other's camp.
But we can be friends ...
Work together, talk together.
Walk together.
One country ...
We can share
So I decide to make something ...
Make a future.

Not watching from behind a tree,
But walking together.

I think this is the best way
So we can share our culture.
White people and Aboriginal people ...
Together.

# JAMES BARRIPANG

Barripang's father was an outstanding leader among the Golpa tribe
and other tribes of the islands in the Wessel Archipelago. The Wessels are not only a
stunning piece of Australia's northern coastline, they hold precious parts of Australia's
Aboriginal heritage, particularly in the cave paintings that document the Aboriginal
contact with the Macassans from the Celebes prior to Cook's voyages of discovery.
Barripang has inherited the primary responsibility for the Golpa territory and
traditions. He lives with his family on Marchinbar Island, hunting and fishing with his
spears as his forefathers did before European contact.

I was born here at Jensen Bay.
Right here in the Wessel Islands
Harry Djinjgulul ... father
He was the King of the Wessels.
I am the eldest son
So I inherit this country,
These sacred places
I will give these things to my sons
All our laws.

My father was born on our country too.
His father too.
My grandfather ...
He died here.
Here in the Wessel Islands.

That was old times when the people used woltha ...
Fish traps.

Long time ago.
When I was a little boy,
My father told me about these caves.
These caves are important to us,
They are special.

Before, my father look after this country.
He always live here,
Hunt here,
Camp here
They always live here.

My grandfather,
My father,
And me.
All the same country,
All the same story.

Cave is important,
It is special for us.

We used to bury our people
Put the body in cave.
Wrap it up in paperbark
Tie it with string
Then put it in cave ...
Finished.

Only men could visit these caves
Not women,
Not children.
They would be killed.
Maybe that was hard
But that was the law.

Law ...
It came from long time ago.
Same as sacred things.
They all came then.

Aborigine can't make law
It came from long time ago.
From the first time.
It can never change.
Always stay the same.

Our culture can never change,
Our law can never change.
Only people change.
They born ...
They die.
But law stays the same.

Each person is responsible for law,
For culture.

The law comes from the beginning ...
What Europeans call history.
But Europeans still change law.
Our law can never change.

My grandfather gave the law to my father.
My father gave it to me ...
Still the same
And now I look after it,
That's my responsibility
Until I pass it on.

The spirit from this land
It will go into my wife
And she will have children
Children from this land.
Then they belong to this country
Spirit of this dreaming.

But when you die,
Spirit will go to heaven.
Spirit can't go to any other place
Because God made us.

If you look after the country ...
Properly,
You got to live on it.
Then your children will be born on it.
The law will stay strong
And culture will never stop.

I'm living on my country
Every day I hunt on it.
Wet season,
Dry season
All the time hunting.
And now I've got a garden too,

*James Barripang's traditional responsibilites for his country and the burial sites found within its caves were inherited from his father*

*Deciduous monsoon forests provide a cool retreat for the Golpa people during the dry season*

Pineapple, cassava, sugarcane, lime,
All these things
Coming up from my country.
That way I don't have to move about
I can build a house.

Old times.
We have to move around
All the time moving.
Every new season
We have again
Mayaltha ...
Flowering season.

103

Midawar ...
Fruiting season
Dharratharramirri
Early dry season.

Each season we move,
New camp ...
New food.

But now we are making a house ...
Proper house that one.
We stay in one place then
But we still have to hunt,
Hunting all around our country
They will know our land
They will know our culture.

Long time ago ...
Before Captain Cook,
We see Macassans
They come with Bärra [northwest wind]
They leave with Bulunu [southeast wind]
We work with them
Catch Nyon [trepang],
We share our food, water everything.
They give us Macassan names.

They come from Macassar ...
Every year,
And some of our old people
They go back too.
Stay there for one year,
Might be stay longer.
Have a look all around.
Then they come home again.

Macassans give us a lot of things
Lipalipa [dugout canoe]
Birrtha [rice]
Ngarali [tobacco]
Lunginy [smoking pipe]
Lots of things.

After that ...
Missionary come along.
Bäpa Sheppy [Reverend Shepherdson]
He was first one.
My father was with him.
He looked after Bäpa Sheppy
Showed him all around this country.

That was war time
Japanese were bombing Milingimbi
Some Aboriginal people ...
Our family,
They were killed by bombs.
That's why missionary come here.

But now we back on our country
Living our law
Looking after our country.

# BIDDY SIMON

## BIRRINDILIL

Biddy is the focus and driving force of the outstation movement among
her people, who have re-established themselves on their traditional country northeast
of Kununurra on the Western Australian border. She has witnessed the degradation
and destruction of her people, many of whom are now dependent on alcohol.
The path leading to the destruction of her people and culture is clear to Biddy.
Equally clear is the path to maintaining and enriching the positive aspects of her
traditional culture, and Biddy is determined to do everything in her power to steer her
people away from destruction and into a better life,
immersed in their traditions.

I am a Kadjerrong woman
Kadjerrong and Murrinbatha mixed
I'm living on Kadjerrong country
Legune Station ...
That's Kadjerrong country.

We got our own outstation there
Marralam we call it.
We living back on the country
Looking after it.
That's the proper way.

We got little bit shed there
Not much money for house
But billabong all round
Beautiful water lilies,
Plenty of tortoise, wild potato
Lot of bush tucker
We got everything there.

Old days used to be only old town,
Old Wyndham that one ...
No Kununurra then.
Aboriginal people living on stations then,
Out in the bush
Then they start to come to town
They find grog then.

Pretty soon lot of people come along town.
All leave the bush,
And then Welfare start to look after them
Plenty of damper and tea
And then they just sit down
Only think for grog then.

Soon they forget about bush,
Just hunting for grog, whisky

And that one you light fire with ...
Metho.

Little bit hang on to law then
But lot of people dying.

We learn from white people
But we learn wrong things.
What we going to teach our kids?
Learn him how to sit down, drink grog?
No law ...
No future.

I want my kids to grow up proper,
Grow up on their country
Then they grow up their kids proper too.
This Kununurra not our country
If we just live here
Our kids can't learn to hunt,
Can't know their country
Can't know their culture.

You look around town
Grandma growing up children
Mothers and fathers not think about kids
Just worry for grog.

I was grow up on Legune Station
My dad buried there.
That's where I been pushing for outstation
Kadjerrong country ...
Proper place to grow up kids.

When old people die
They want their bones to go back ...
Back to their country.
That good for spirit,
But too late for kids.

*ABOVE: Biddy Simon has a strong commitment to educate the young in the Kadjerrong traditions*

*RIGHT: The billabongs in Kadjerrong country abound with water lilies, a staple food source*

Only one place you can learn bush life ...
In the bush.
That's why I work for outstation.
That our country.

Government help with money for outstation,
But we build it ourself.
Money from mining ...
We get vehicle with that.
All this help us to hang on to country.

If you gonna hang on to country,
If you gonna teach your kids,
You gotta live on your country.
You gotta look after it.

## BIDDY SIMON

If you sit down in town,
Whose law you teach?
Your kids won't learn country.
They might get spoiled.
Granny gotta grow up them kids.
But kids watch parents.
If parents sit down,
All the time look after grog,
Then kids grow up just the same as them.

Parents gotta look after their own baby,
Like my parents.
They grow me up longa bush.
All the time look after me.
Teach me.

My dad was Murrinbatha man.
And my mum ...
They all the time look after me.
Grow me up in Murrinbatha and Kadjerrong
country.

My father run that country
He was boss for all round Legune.
Table Hill near Port Keats,
All across coast to Turtle Point near Keep River ...
Murrinbatha, Kadjerrong right up to Dhulbung
country.

We are close related,
And all us women look after law together
Old Ruby Tooboolin, Daisy Carlton, Daisy Djundun
We all look after law for women.

Kids can't learn law in town,
Can't learn country in town.
That's why we got outstation.

If you stay in town all the time
Then just animals looking after country.

Flagon, carton, can ...
That new culture growing up.
Your mate give you one can
Then you might be part of that mob too.
That grog is new law for them
And that holding them back from country.
Only one sacred site for that mob ...
Grog shop.
Only one totem ...
White can.

First time white people come
We all been fight ...
Lot of people die.
Then we work along station, mission.

Welfare days after that ...
We gotta live in town.
Too many people just sit down
Tea, damper, grog.

That should be finished now.
We gotta work for country,
Look after law,
Grow up our kids.

We can talk for ourselves now
Talk to government,
Work with mining company.
Now we got a future.